My Rock Pool

written by Anne Giulieri

photography by Ned Meldrum

To make a rock pool you will need: some *card*, some blue *cellophane*, a *box*, *string*, *tape* and *scissors*.

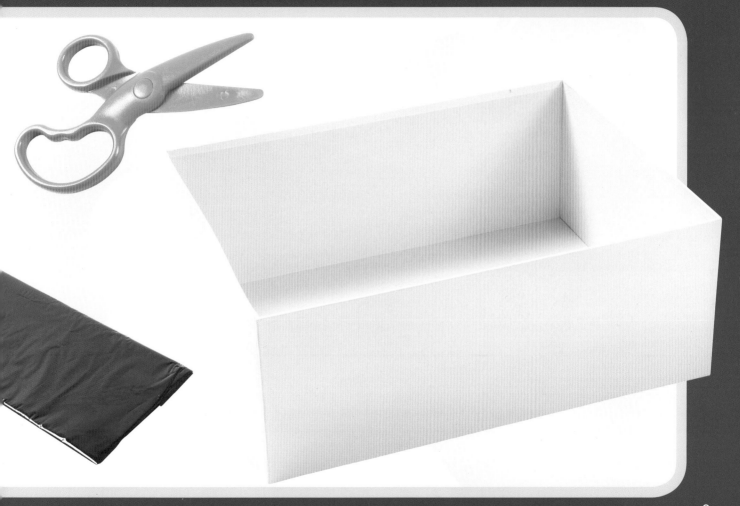

There are lots of sea animals
you can put into your rock pool.

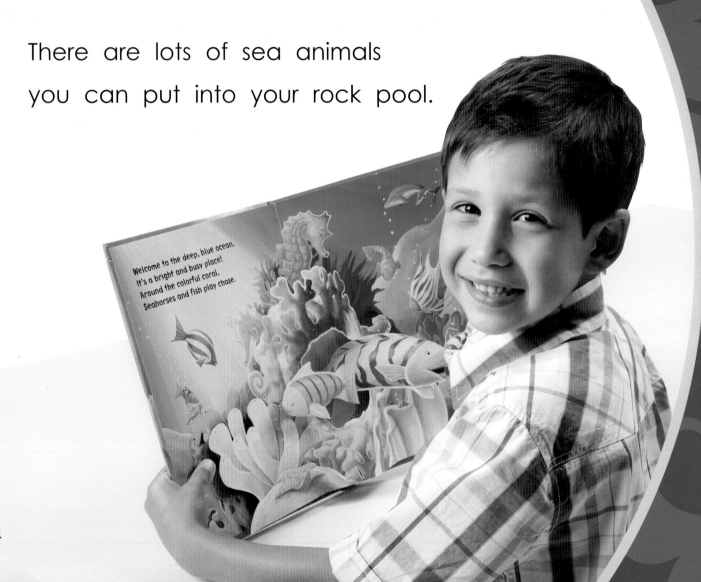

Welcome to the deep, blue ocean,
It's a bright and busy place!
Around the colorful coral,
Seahorses and fish play chase.

You can make a *sea horse*, a *starfish*, a *fish* and a *crab*.

You need to make the rock pool first.

To make your rock pool get a box.

Put the box onto its side.

Cut out the blue cellophane.
Put it on the inside of the box,
so that it looks like the sea.

You can also cut out strips of blue cellophane.

Stick the strips on the box,

so that it looks like the sea.

Then cut out some *rocks* from brown card.
Put the rocks around the box,
so that it looks like a rock pool.

To make your sea animals,
you need to get some card.
Cut out a crab and a fish.
You can also cut out a starfish
and a sea horse.

You will need to make a tiny *hole*
in all of your sea animals.
Put the string on like this.

Make some tiny holes in the top of the box.

Put the string into the holes.

Your rock pool is now ready.

The string makes your sea animals go up and down.
It will look like they are swimming in your rock pool.

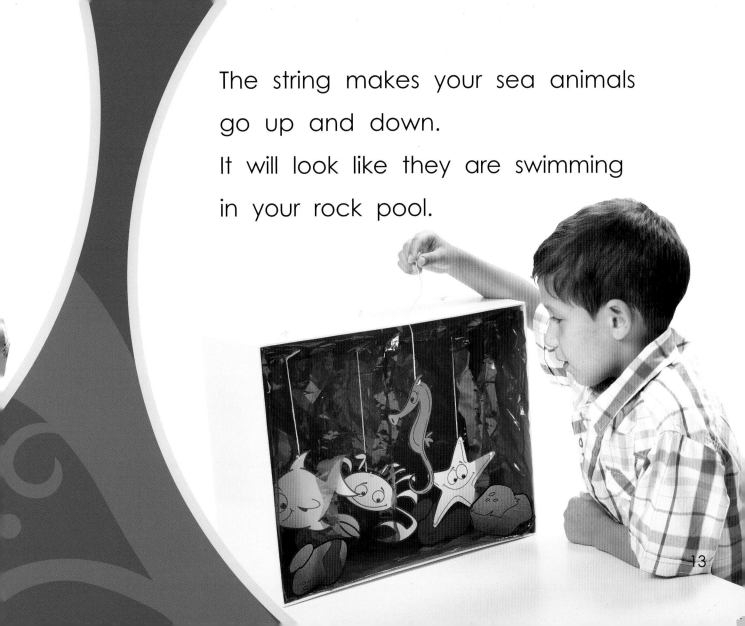

You can make lots of sea animals for your rock pool.

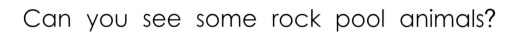

Can you see some rock pool animals?

Picture Glossary

box

fish

sea horse

card

hole

starfish

cellophane

rocks

string

crab

scissors

tape